This book is to be returned on or
before the last date stamped below.

OR 6.1.93

YESTERDAY

A Photographic Album of Daily Life in Britain

1953-1970

YESTERDAY

A Photographic Album of Daily Life in Britain

1953-1970

Introduced by

Benny Green

J. M. Dent & Sons Ltd
London Melbourne Toronto

First published 1982
Introduction © J. M. Dent & Sons Ltd
Picture selection and text © John Topham Picture Library 1982
Picture 120 © BBC
Picture 142 © S & G Press Agency

This book is set in 9/10½ point VIP Rockwell Light by
D. P. Media Ltd, Hitchin, Herts
Printed in Great Britain by
BAS Printers Ltd, Stockbridge, Hants, for
J. M. Dent & Sons Ltd
Aldine House, 33 Welbeck Street, London W1M 8LX

British Library Cataloguing in Publication Data

Yesterday: photographs of daily life 1953–1970
   Great Britain – Social life and customs – 20th
   century – Pictorial works
   941.085′0222   DA566.4

   ISBN 0-460-04549-0

Contents

Introduction

One time, there was a musician of my acquaintance who invented a new parlour game. What you did was to get yourself photographed from the same vantage point every Monday morning of your life. Then, on your seventieth birthday you gathered all the shots together in chronological order, flicked them through and watched yourself grow old. When the game was first described to me, at the start of the period covered by this volume, I was young enough to laugh about it. Now I am not so sure. I study the photographs in this collection and I perceive the march of time, pushing back my hair-line, stamping the crow's feet around the eyes, making painful adjustments to ligament and tendon. The images flicker: the Coronation, Suez, teddy boys and skinheads, hula hoops and Tony Hancock, Marilyn and Brigitte, flower folk and the Wind of Change, Aldermaston and Vietnam, Bobby Moore and Basil D'Oliveira, Home in, Wilson in, Heath in, hemlines up, hemlines down, hemlines up again, punctured skylines overhung by Concorde, a tight little island feeling the pinch as the planet contracts.

It can be an arduous business, comprising part of history. I spent most of the 1950s playing the saxophone for a living in precisely the kind of dance halls, jazz clubs and concert rooms glimpsed in this collection, venues embellished by the beehive coiffeur and the winklepickered foot. Some of the scenes preserved by the click of the shutter are so familiar to me that I scrutinize the faces in the crowd in the half-expectation of finding my younger self staring incuriously out at me from behind the impenetrable palisades of time past. I spent Coronation night, 1953, in a woebegone dance hall in Worksop, dispensing 'Secret Love' and 'Zing a Little Zong' to celebrants who had very little idea what they were celebrating. Every one of us on the premises that tipsy night, performers as well as customers, was young enough and callow enough to assume that the new reign would be just like the old one – except that for the first time in our experience the reigning monarch, instead of being a whiskered Edwardian patriarch, or some totemic middle-aged gentleman, would be young enough to grow old alongside us. A novel like *1984* still sounded futuristic enough to qualify as science fiction. In all the great cities there stretched mile upon square mile of huddled homes built in the Victorian heyday. Those homes, the streets and alleys and squares they formed, the domestic conventions they represented, had survived two world wars, five different monarchs and how many indifferent politicians

masquerading as statesmen? The delicate equipoise of urban communal life remained undisturbed. My paternal grandfather moved into his Marylebone backwater in 1902, and left it feet first fifty years later. He may have gone to his fathers, but the building endured. Why should anyone assume that anything fundamental would ever change?

Of course there were noises about bringing in the brave new world, but then again, when it came to politics, prosperity seemed always to be just around the corner. Yet the thirty years of radical change which followed turned out, I do believe, to be the most difficult the British had ever had to live with. The period began with the touching flurry of a post-imperial euphoria. The Festival of Britain had seemed triumphantly to assert something or other, although you never seemed to come across anyone who could tell you exactly what it was. But hadn't the Great Exhibition of 1851 symbolized a softening of social asperities and the dawn of a great period of expansion and prosperity? Why not again? There was heady talk of the New Elizabethans, bold latterday conquistadores usually depicted in the ads as sturdy young air pilots or naval officers with spade beards, gallantly toasting their own health in smart bars. The flummery of empire may have modulated into the minor tonality of Commonwealth co-operation, but the British continued to regard themselves as a Great Power which still kept up a presence, still showed the flag. Even as the old outposts of empire – Aden, Cyprus, Malaya, Uganda, Tanganyika – slipped away towards alien destinies, there survived the old Palmerstonian belief that no matter where you found yourself in this troubled old world, a British passport still stood for something. In the event, it was obliged to stand for plenty.

A mental image forms of the imperial chicken running round in ever-decreasing diplomatic circles, pathetically unaware that the double-edged sword of history has already lopped its head off. The first twitches of posthumous panic were not long in coming. One evening in the late summer of 1956, I was sitting in the box of a theatre in Shaftesbury Avenue with some musician friends watching one of those touchingly archaic revues concerned with amateur operatic productions, bridge parties, film stars and the weather. When we emerged into the outside world, it was to find the streets humming with the news of an assault on the Suez Canal by a conspiratorial group which included the British. The coup failed. A few American platitudes, apparently composed by a convocation of retarded movie moguls, casually swept the British lion into the dustbin, and the rest of the world had a good laugh. There followed a few moving choruses of woe and lamentation from the liberal conscience, which was so scandalized by this amazing act of aggrandizement that it demonstrated the old Dunkirk spirit by actually changing newspapers. But the real unease was rooted in the perception of the degree of footling incompetence of the crime. Naked aggression is bad enough, but bungled naked aggression is

not to be borne. The British began to wake up to the alarming possibility that history was leaving them behind.

The disgrace and fiasco of Suez could only have happened under a dormouse administration, but the rest of the nation seemed lively enough. Concurrent with Suez was the emergence of a number of Angry Young Men, who wrote autobiographical plays and books loosely disguised as philosophy or polemic, and which were said by the middle classes to express the frustrations of the working classes. The latter, however, were pursuing their own delights, which included anglicized editions of Elvis Presley, a dawning realization of the possibilities of the long-playing record, and a determination to look different which resulted in a vast army of young people who looked perfectly alike. There began to be talk of a new phenomenon called The Generation Gap, which meant disagreeing with your old man. The young British male, depressed and baffled by the looming shadow of conscription, began to betray peacock tendencies previously unknown. Your haircut replaced your hat as an issue of cosmic importance; perfume for men cunningly disguised as aftershave, began infiltrating from America; jewelry gradually lost its exclusive femininity. Happy is the land so preoccupied with fashion. Admittedly a few Jeremiahs issued warnings about the evils of advertising, which had found a new stronghold in the recently opened commercial television channel, and one or two economists tried to say something about world markets without making themselves intelligible to the population at large, or even to each other. People told themselves that the more things changed, the more they stayed the same. There was much to support this notion. In that summer of 1956 the Victorians were still well in evidence. In May I awoke in the musicians' block of a south coast holiday camp one morning to read of the death of that relic from the Naughty Nineties, Sir Max Beerbohm; not long afterwards Walter de la Mare followed him. But Masefield was still Poet Laureate, J. B. Priestley was still churning them out. England had retained the Ashes thanks partly to Denis Compton. In California the Metro-Goldwyn executive Arthur Freed had been quoted as saying that 'television will never take the place of the movies'. Life, it seemed, was life, and that was that. Daily existence continued to be recognizable as the same one the British had been living throughout the century.

Of course there was air travel and the continental holiday, which gave the masses for the first time a practical interest in rates of currency exchange, and struck fear into the hearts of a thousand chatelaines of seaside Mon Reposes and Seaviews. There was the belated introduction into Britain of the motorway. There appeared to be an increase in the number of divorces. But were not these things unmixed blessings, harbingers of self-expression, democracy, personal freedom? At least the British could pride themselves on possessing an enviable degree of personal liberty. To prove it there was the rubber hammer of television satire, which now began

bouncing playfully off the heads of the panjandrums of the Macmillan era. And most impressive of all, there were the great public rows, scandals, arguments, dust-ups, exposures, which seemed to have become a regular feature of life. What nation dared to air its opinions, to hammer out its convictions, to exercise its ethics, so vociferously as the British? Where else could a man stand up and say exactly what he wanted in words which seemed to him to be the most appropriate words? So impassioned and so wonderfully comic were most of these rows that it escaped general notice that in any reasonably sane society the issues involved would either have been quietly settled years ago or already had been by the sheer power of general usage.

There was, for example, the extraordinary business of Lady Chatterley, at whose trial in 1960 was solemnly debated the issue of whether English society could afford to acknowledge on the printed page the fact that people not only had genitals but actually referred to them in a variety of ways. The assorted legal hirelings who fought the battle conducted themselves as though so aloof from the rough-and-tumble of procreation as to have been the outcome of a series of brilliant immaculate conceptions. But there was a slapstick sense in which the trial was bogus and those who had insisted upon it a bunch of noodles. For whatever its outcome, the frequency with which genitals would appear in print would remain unaffected. All the trial debated was the legal sanction for the printing of these words, which was quite another matter. Just as in America the Volstead Act concerning prohibition had labelled a national habit illegal without remotely affecting anyone's determination to go on indulging in it, so the puritans who put Lady Chatterley in the dock apparently believed that if they outlawed her, printed genitals would go away.

Meanwhile the general public, healthily Rabelaisian in these affairs, howled with mirth to watch what were sometimes laughingly referred to as its betters making so spectacular an exhibition of themselves. But then the British Establishment had never been much good when it came to Sex. Not so long after the Chatterley case had subsided, there rose up another, the Profumo Affair, in which a Minister of the Crown was said to have imperilled national security by indulging in the time-honoured custom known to the workers as pulling birds. Ribaldry hung on the air as revelations about the Misses Keeler and Rice Davies were circulated, and Mr Profumo, his career in pieces, found himself consigned to the company of those two Victorian Charlies, Parnell and Dilke, men whose promise was betrayed by the flash of a petticoat, as the saying goes. But it wasn't so much what Mr Profumo did that cost him his future, as what he said about it. What had *really* upset his political peers was the fact that he had actually told a lie in Parliament. The British public received this news in sceptical silence, having understandably reached the conclusion a long time ago that most political careers are in jeopardy only if their owners tell the truth in Parliament.

With two such colourful extravaganzas did the Swinging Sixties get under way. Licence gathered pace daily, and in its wake came licentiousness. A theatre critic spoke a four-letter word on a live television show. Censorship was routed. Homosexuality and abortion laws were amended. Betting shops and sex cinemas became legal. Capital punishment was ended. The new aristocracy of pop stars, hairdressers, fashion designers and photographers quickly established itself. Prostitution was swept off the streets up to the first floor, which raised not only its altitude but its linguistic tone, because ladies began resorting to whimsical euphemism in advertising their services; suddenly the market was flooded by a surplus of large chests, French teachers and practitioners of the arts of erection and demolition. British life became the wonder of the world, or at least so said the British press. The England football team won the World Cup and perhaps also an election for the Labour Party; later, when the team lost the World Cup, people said it had also lost an election for the Labour Party.

The collapse into reality was not very far away now. Soon there would be problems of race, of violence in the streets, of unemployment, of soaring inflation. The very nation itself would disclose fissiparous tendencies never dreamed of by the imperialists even in the dark night of the soul, with the Scottish Home Rule movement becoming a political reality and Welsh insurgents firing English holiday homes. In the doltishly dubbed Swinging Sixties, none of these nightmares had arrived, but there were one or two straws in the wind, and a few people were beginning to wonder. For one thing, there was the business of the British Secret Service. It gradually transpired that that entire organization appeared to have been working for the Other Side. As defection followed revelation, and disclosure followed rumour, a sensitive ear might have detected a distant but ominous whirring noise which eventually proved to be the corpse of poor John Buchan turning in its grave. As for the Irish Question, that ancient issue which for long periods of recent history had seemed to find a Gladstonian quiescence, it was once again threatening to become the same old suppurating wound in the British body politic.

Which photographs reflect these profound and unimagined changes most dramatically of all? Perhaps the shots registering the rise of a new consumer-group, the teenagers, with their own music, fashion, design, publishing, politics, morality? Or is it the glimpse of Bertrand Russell fighting for a future he knows he will never live to share, the face of the Enlightenment, looking remarkably like the Mad Hatter, grimly confronting the prospect of holocaust? My own choice may seem frivolous, but only because great events are often presaged by the smallest incidents. Turn to the shot of Roger Bannister completing the first four-minute mile in history. Study that homely scene and ask in which ways it might have looked different had it happened a generation later. The runner, it will be perceived, carries no endorsements on his vest. The man at the tape, having put aside his old-fashioned handbell, is studying a hand-held, hand-operated watch, and has taken his eyes off the runner at the very moment when the feet are about to cross the line. The house in the background belies any hint of a great stadium. There is no sign of the paraphernalia of television. Today that group of quaintly Burberried men would have been swept aside by uniformed officialdom. The microclocks of the computer age would have measured Bannister's time infinitely more accurately than the course approximation of 3.59.4. The event would have been witnessed, at the moment it was happening, by a worldwide audience of anything up to 500,000,000, most of whom would have received their pictures by kind permission of a satellite suspended in the Wellsian void. Overnight, Bannister's name would have been toasted in Kenya, in Ethiopia, in Finland, and wherever else there has grown up a profound understanding of the philosophy of footracing. Most revealing of all, that race, if it were to mean much to the groundlings of the 1980s, would have had to be more than ten seconds faster.

If I see something allegorical in those contrasts, it is not simply because I spent some of the sweetest moments of adolescence galloping round running tracks, but because the circumstances in which even the most dedicated amateur performs his deeds today, in whatever sphere, are shaped by the forces of communication, forces which can bestow instant if qualified immortality. It is not a world to which the British find it easy to adjust, having been conditioned by the usage of centuries to a more leisurely pace even than the one Bannister achieved on that sensational morning in 1954. In searching for an appropriate dying fall to these reflections, I can do no better than quote the words of the chronicler of empire, Jan Morris: 'It was time the Empire went, but it was sad to see it go'. In these photographs, we do indeed see it go. As to what takes its place in the life of the British, only the next volume in this series will reveal. And at the time of going to press, the relevant photographs remain in the darkroom of history.

Benny Green

The New Elizabethan Age

1
Smiling happily, Queen
Elizabeth II rides in the golden
State Coach into Buckingham
Palace at the end of her
triumphant procession from
her Coronation at Westminster
Abbey on 2 June 1953. She
wears the Imperial State
Crown and carries the Royal
Sceptre and Orb.

2
Over 1,000,000 overseas
visitors were in London for the
Coronation, and 25,000,000
people watched the ceremony
on television. For the first time
the monarch could be said to
have been crowned, as the
Prayer Book puts it, in the sight
of all the people. A young
Elizabethan here watches the
Queen leave Westminster
Abbey after a rehearsal on 26
May 1953.

3
With immaculate timing, one
news story broke on
Coronation day itself– in a
British expedition led by
Colonel John Hunt, New
Zealander Edmund Hillary
(pictured here) and Nepalese
Sherpa Tensing had stood on
the peak of Mount Everest, the
first men to do so.

4
The enthusiasm for the new Queen went on and on. As she arrives at Benson House, Kennington, London, in July 1955, a woman behind the youngsters makes the most of her opportunity to take a photograph that will always be treasured.

5
Admiring onlookers gathered wherever the new Queen and the Royal Family went – for instance outside the New Theatre, London, where, on 4 August 1955, the Queen and Princess Margaret accompanied the Queen Mother on her birthday to see 'The Remarkable Mr Pennypacker'.

6
Antony Armstrong-Jones's
photograph of the Royal Family
in 1957 was taken by the lake in
the grounds of Buckingham
Palace. Charles was then nine
and Anne seven.

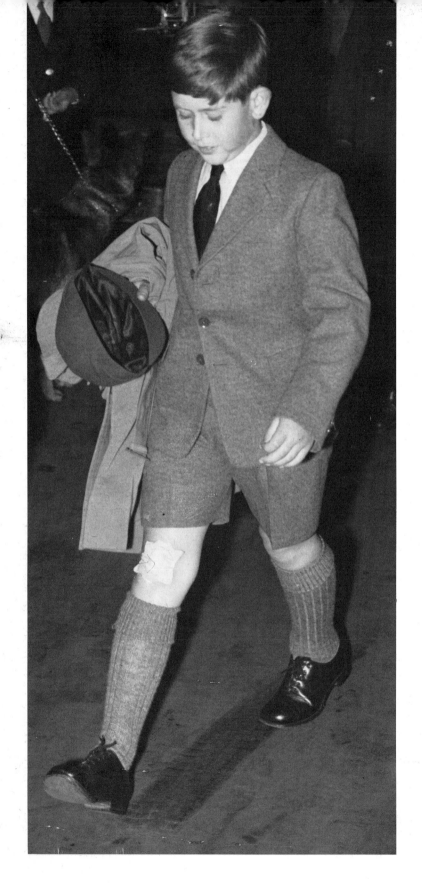

7
Prince Charles was to have as normal an education as was possible for the heir to the throne. On 22 September 1958 he left, sticking plaster and all, by train from Paddington Station to begin the new term at Cheam School in Berkshire.

8
The message and inspiration of the Queen reached the people easily through the new media. Tables were cleared of Christmas dinner throughout the land by 2.55 pm sharp, and in 1958, with stoned dates and Meltis New Berry Fruits close to hand, her subjects could see the Queen darkly on a television screen.

9
Queen Elizabeth and Prince
Philip backstage at 'My Fair
Lady' at the Drury Lane
Theatre, talking with its star,
Rex Harrison, 5 May 1958.
Co-stars Julie Andrews and
Stanley Holloway look on.

10
Dame Margot Fonteyn was the
prima ballerina of the Royal
Ballet when Queen Elizabeth
and Prince Philip attended the
gala performance of opera and
ballet on 10 June 1958, to mark
the centenary of the Royal
Opera House, Covent Garden.

11
On 4 April 1955 Queen
Elizabeth dined with her Prime
Minister, Sir Winston Churchill,
at 10 Downing Street, the
evening before he retired.

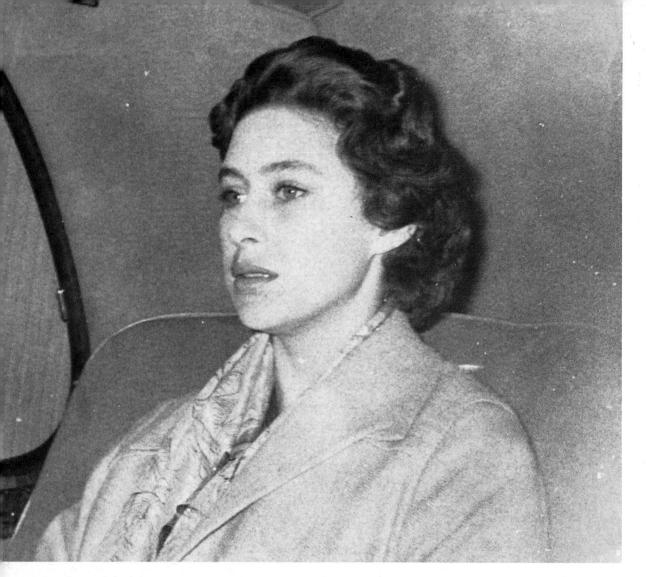

12

In October 1955, mindful of the church's teaching that marriage is indissoluble, Princess Margaret announced that she would not marry Group Captain Peter Townsend, the innocent party of a divorce.

13

On the day that Princess Margaret and her husband, Antony Armstrong-Jones, returned from their Caribbean honeymoon in 1960, his waxwork effigy was stolen from Madame Tussauds and was later found lurking in a telephone kiosk in Savoy Hill, Westminster.

14
July 1954 – Noël Coward and
Marlene Dietrich together in
the most expensive suite in
town – the Penthouse at the
Dorchester Hotel. Noël
Coward had organized a
charity show, 'Night of a
Hundred Stars', with Dietrich
as its leading attraction.

15
'The Sex Kitten', Brigitte
Bardot, in London in April 1959,
for location scenes for a new film.

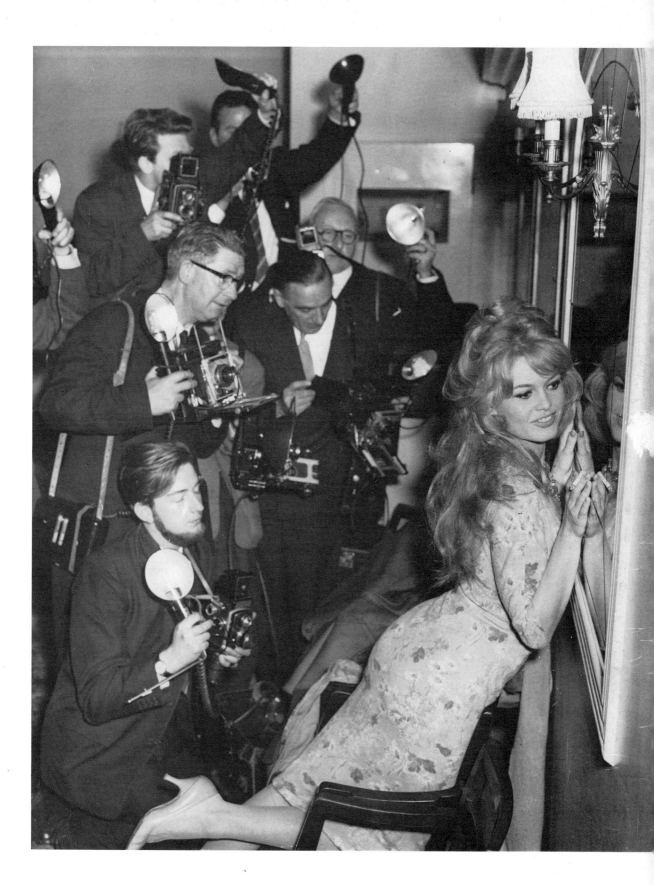

◄ 16
Diana Dors – in polka-dots – at London Airport, July 1959.

► 17
Sabrina – Britain's answer to Jayne Mansfield – poses for cameramen at the Park Lane Hotel in 1955.

▼ 18
Having sought political asylum in Britain, twenty-three-year-old Russian ballet star, Rudolf Nureyev, made his London début in Dame Margot Fonteyn's gala matinée, attended by Princess Marina of Kent, at Drury Lane, 2 November 1961.

19
At Oxford on 6 May 1954, Roger Bannister became the first man to run the mile in less than four minutes. A twenty-five-year-old medical student, Bannister's time was 3 minutes 59.4 seconds.

20
Gordon Richards rode Sir Victor Sassoon's horse, Pinza, to victory in the 1953 Derby, four lengths ahead of the Queen's horse, Aureole.

21
The Comet was the first aircraft to start a scheduled jet service for British Overseas Airways Corporation (BOAC), bringing the countries of the Commonwealth considerably closer together and giving Britain a dramatic lead in the aviation industry. An all-party group of MPs prepare to board.

24
Many small village schools could not cope with the educational needs of the new Elizabethans, and this one in the Weald of Kent, on 31 June 1953, was typical of those that were to close.

25
At Woodbrook Junior Training Centre, Bromley, as at so many new schools, television began to be used in lessons, children often giving it more attention than they gave to their teachers.

26

Comprehensive schools
started in London in 1951 and
the first, Kidbrooke, was called
variously 'a palace of learning'
and 'a sausage machine'.
Crown Woods School, Eltham,
had 2000 pupils and boasted a
boarding section intended
primarily for children of
members of the forces
overseas. Beneath photographs
of the new folk heroes of the
age, twelve-year-old Robert
Rouse of Lee Green plays chess
with David Simons, whose
parents were in Libya.

27

In the 1950s, before the building
of the new universities, Britain
had fewer universities in proportion
to its population than any other
European country, but Oxford
and Cambridge were inter-
national centres of excellence.
At Balliol College, Oxford, an
undergraduate invites friends
to his room for after-lunch coffee:
l–r Nils Astrup of Oslo,
Michael McNevin of Chicago,
Hans Sluga of Bonn, the host,
the Hon Oliver James, son of the
Vice-Chancellor of York
University, and Edward Mortimer,
son of the Bishop of Exeter.

28
For those who did not stay in higher education there was no lack of work. One employer (perhaps a former army sergeant?) struggled to maintain standards against a rising tide of teenage culture.

29
Teenagers with money to spare often spent a lot of it on their hair: this was part of the regular Saturday afternoon queue in Hounslow for a styling, shampoo and wave set in 1953.

30
Young gallants in their 'Edwardian suits' go into a dreamy two-step at a London dance hall in 1954. When the opportunity offered they launched into a 'hot' jive 'during which the girls were swung around'.

31
Soft drinks, potato crisps and fags were all that was needed for a night out.

32
Test-your-weight machines were popular for a generation which suddenly started to pay the penalty for increased affluence and leisure.

33
Overcrowding in small houses
and flats was a growing social
problem in the 1950s. Here
breakfast is cooked on a
primus, the kettle boils on a
heater and the clothes dry
overhead.

34
In 1953, forty-two-year-old Tom Fail, Northumberland coal miner, one of Britain's 700,000 miners, lived in a comfortable five-roomed cottage with his wife and ten-year-old son. Although standards of living were improving for many workers, Tom's average weekly pay packet of £15 still meant that thrift was the order of the day.

35
According to *Illustrated* magazine, 1954, 'Patrick Welsh and his family are among the lucky tenants to be allocated a flat on the top (11th) floor of the new skyscraper flats which have been erected by the local council in Gee Street, Finsbury. The flat has three bedrooms, a living room, kitchen and bathroom with constant hot water, and background heating. It costs £2 5s. 9d. a week but the Welshes say that the fresh air and the birds make it feel like living on the sea front.

36
New towns and housing estates
were built around the old
towns, often reinforcing family
and social ties. 'Everyone likes
the new set-up', said Mrs Marie
Thompson, pictured here. 'I
seldom have to worry about
baby-sitters.'

37
Smart houses for the upwardly
mobile middle class were built
in the countryside. 'Edward
and his family can relax in the
living area knowing they are
not overlooked by other
houses'. Photographed for
Woman magazine in 1958.

38
Into Southampton in 1954 come
another 130 immigrants from
the West Indies, gathering in
the bows of the ship, prior to
stepping ashore at
Southampton to undergo the
routine check by Passport and
Customs Officials. Their assets
were a few pounds in their
pockets – and a touching faith
in Great Britain.

39
In October 1959, under a 'no waiting' sign, Gurbaja Singh sits on his luggage at Victoria Station, London, after being given permission to enter Britain. By 1964 over 1,000,000 immigrants had arrived in postwar Britain and entry was being restricted.

40
A West Indian ticket collector goes about his daily business in a London bus – one of 8,000 coloured workers employed in public transport in 1958.

41
An efficient nation was a healthy nation. A class of five- and six-year-olds undergo exercises on special apparatus at the Hungerford School, King's Cross, London, 1954.

42
Some of the New Elizabethans at Bluecoat School, Manchester, hold out their hands in the traditional inspection for cleanliness before every meal.

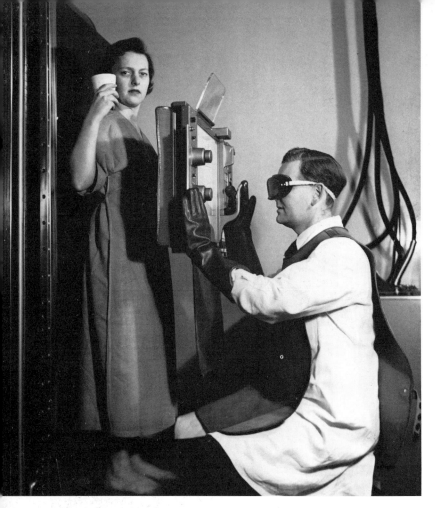

43
Regular health check-ups and x-rays were encouraged in the 1950s. This is the X-ray Department of Westminster Hospital, London, in March 1957.

44
A type of influenza, originating in the Far East, reached Britain in 1957. The Royal Army Medical Corps worked at the World Influenza Centre at Mill Hill together with the Wright-Fleming Institute, St Mary's Hospital, London, to identify the virus and develop a vaccine to combat 'Asian flu'.

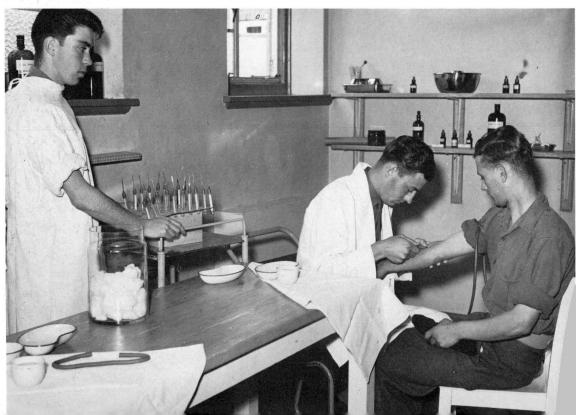

45

Another great scourge, poliomyelitis, was tackled by preventitive medicine. A mobile vaccination van was part of the anti-polio campaign. Factory workers line up for treatment at the Mobile Immunization Clinic, Cossor House, London, in September 1959.

46

The new and the old begin to meet. Children skip in a street near the Mersey river beneath the completed arch of the £3,000,000 Mersey bridge, then the third largest span in the world, linking Lancashire and Cheshire. It was opened by Princess Alexandra of Kent on 21 July 1961.

47
One clean, cheerful New
Elizabethan, appeared in
Woman's Realm on 2 January
1960, accompanied by an
uplifting poem from Lily Dean:

Pretend that you are happy,
Though your spirits may be low
Wear a cheerful face, and sing
A little as you go.

Pretence like this is courage,
Spreading sunshine on your way,
And you'll often find the effort
Clears your troubles right away.

Twist and Shout

48
Skiffle at Brighton in the 1950s.

53
Cliff Richard– one of the most durable stars from the late 1950s– in an early concert with the Shadows.

54
Adam Faith in 1961, with his silver disc to mark the quarter-million sales of his recording of 'Lonely Pup'.

55

The twist, all the way from the
Peppermint Orange in New
York, swept Britain in the early
1960s. Over 1200 twisters
crossed the Channel on the
Royal Daffodil in 1962, dancing
non-stop throughout the
twelve-hour journey from
Southend to Calais. Ten bands
provided the music and when
the exhausted twisters arrived
in Calais they were met by
extra French police and
special barricades.

56
A Soho coffee bar was more popular with young people than a pub which had to be shared with the older generation.

57
'Fortunes are made in Britain's new coffee houses', reported *John Bull* magazine in 1955; 'imaginative fancy has inspired the decoration. They use bamboo and bizarre shapes; one even had the sound of jungle drums.'

58
Gerry and the Pacemakers
perform in the now-famous
Cavern Club, Liverpool, 1964.

59

(a) The sound which transformed a whole generation was the 'Liverpool beat'. Four lads from Liverpool, the Beatles, were soon earning more than the Prime Minister.
(b) In 1964 Harold Wilson presented them with the Show Business Personality Award of the year. From left: Ringo Starr, John Lennon, George Harrison, Paul McCartney.

60

The Beatles in blue – hoodwinking fans massed outside the Hippodrome in Birmingham in 1963 by driving up to the stage door in a police van, disguised as policemen.

61–5

Beatlemania. **61**: teenage fans stand in the pouring rain outside the Adelphi cinema in Slough, November 1963. **62**: part of the chorus of screaming girls who welcomed the Beatles on their return from America in September 1964. **63**: many fans were overcome with exhaustion and hysteria at the premiere of the Beatles' film *Help* in London in July 1965. **64**: police had their work cut out to restrain thousands of fans who besieged the railings of Buckingham Palace as the Beatles were presented with the MBE for services to exports. **65**: the dawn chorus at London airport after another highly successful tour of America, August 1966.

66

In January 1965, *Playboy*
magazine, daring reading in
the permissive age, invited
their contributing editor, Paul
Getty, to lunch to meet Ringo
Starr. For some reason Mr
Getty does not seem to be
enjoying the experience.

67
In 1968 the Beatles opened their London shop, Apple, with a large graphic painting around the clothes boutique. Outraged local shopkeepers forced it to be painted out, disappointing tourists who flocked to see it.

68
Nine-year-old teeny-bopper, Derri Thomas, with her Beatle poster.

70
The staying power of Rock 'n'
Roll was amazing. Bill Haley
was not soon forgotten, and as
late as April 1968 he was still
teaching mini-skirted
youngsters to Rock Around the
Clock.

69
Following hard on the heels of
the Beatles came the Rolling
Stones, providing a more
raucous note in the pop music
world. Here they stroll in
London's Green Park before a
coast-to-coast American tour in
1967. The marks of success lie,
left to right, on: Charlie Watts,
Bill Wyman, Mick Jagger, Keith
Richard and Brian Jones.

71
Signs of the times – the Jimmy
Hendrix record 'Electric Lady
Land' had 21 nude girls on the
sleeve, and 'Go-Go' models
danced to promote it in the
window of I Was Lord
Kitchener's Valet in Piccadilly
Circus, London. John Paul, the
owner, has words with a
policeman, 6 November 1968.

Top Gear

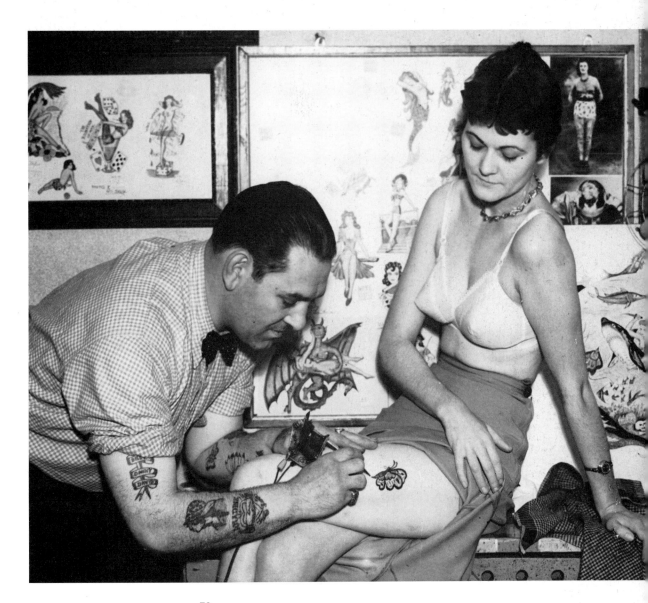

72
Twenty-six-year-old Betty
Coles receives a fashionable
butterfly tattoo from expert
tattooist, Les Skuse, in Bristol,
1953.

73
After wartime austerity and rationing British designers revelled in designs using lots of material. On the steps of Broadcasting House, London, in 1953, model Sheila Wilson arranges the long train of a Digby Morton full evening dress, as photographer David Olins waits in the background.

74
Teddy boys (twins?) with bootlace ties in the 1950s.

75
Formal dress still for the cameraman during the Queen's State Opening of Parliament, 3 November 1964.

76
In March 1964 the Beatle image was on the stocking. The stockings cost 8s. 11d., were available in black or brown, and in the pack was a signed photograph of the four lads.

77
The 'no sides bra' and
see-through look of 1965.

78
Daring, dashing and one of the
most recognizable symbols of
the Sixties– mini-skirts were
turning heads everywhere.

79
On 3 November 1966 the Oxford Union debated 'That this House believes the mini-skirt does not go far enough'. Twenty-year-old Marina Warner wanted it up: Emma Rothschild wanted it down. Five Union members show which side they are on.

80
A fashion model off to work in the King's Road.

81
Mary Quant – one of the
leading London designers of
the 1960s – who helped to
revolutionize fashion for the
young.

82
Top fashion designer Jean
Muir, photographed in 1969,
was considered to produce the
best English clothes of the
period, classically simple and
elegant – and very expensive.

83
The workshop of Zandra
Rhodes, in Notting Hill,
London, 1969. She designed for
the hippy generation and
specialized in fantasy clothing
which had great appeal in
America.

84
Top model Twiggy and her
manager Justin de Villeneuve
outside Harrods, London,
December 1966, waiting for a
taxi. Twiggy's thin, almost
emaciated shape dominated
the line of the period.

85
Jean Shrimpton— 'the Shrimp'—
in 1967; her waif-like face
featured prominently in the
fashion pages of countless
newspapers and magazines.

86
Inside Tommy Roberts's
pop-art clothing boutique, Mr
Freedom, in High Street,
Kensington, London, 1970. The
belt is a *trompe l'oeil*; it is
actually painted on the
garment in the Walt Disney
style.

87
King's Road, Chelsea, London,
was a fashion parade in itself. A
man wears a 'flower-power'
dress there in the 1960s. Mick
Jagger started the fashion
when he brought a dress from
the designer, Mr Fish.

88
A startled-looking Chelsea
pensioner, in his fashionable
uniform, scuttles across the
King's Road.

89
Tourists in 1966 stare at new
male fashions in Carnaby
Street. Carnaby Street later
became a pedestrian precinct,
and was perhaps even better
known than the King's Road.

90
Show jumper and debutante
Jayne Harris, the girl on the left,
was turned away from the
enclosure at Ascot in 1968 in a
trouser suit but made it back in
a mini-skirt.

91
The search for novelty was
desperate. The see-through
dress raised both eyebrows
and temperatures.
Sixteen-year-old Sue Rees,
working on the forecourt of the
Silverstone Garage, Finchley,
London, on 21 June 1968, was
booked by the police for
alleged indecent behaviour.

92
The 'antique' clothes blend harmoniously with the antiques being offered to customers in Portobello Road market, 1967.

93
For people exhausted by novelty, Biba's in High Street, Kensington, 1970, derived its elegance and appeal from the styles of the '20s and '30s.

94
Britain's fashions would not
have run in top gear without the
work of brilliant photographers
who became stars in their own
right. David Bailey married
French film star, Catherine
Deneueve, on 18 August 1965 at
St Pancras Town Hall, London.
Mick Jagger of the Rolling
Stones was best man.

Time Off

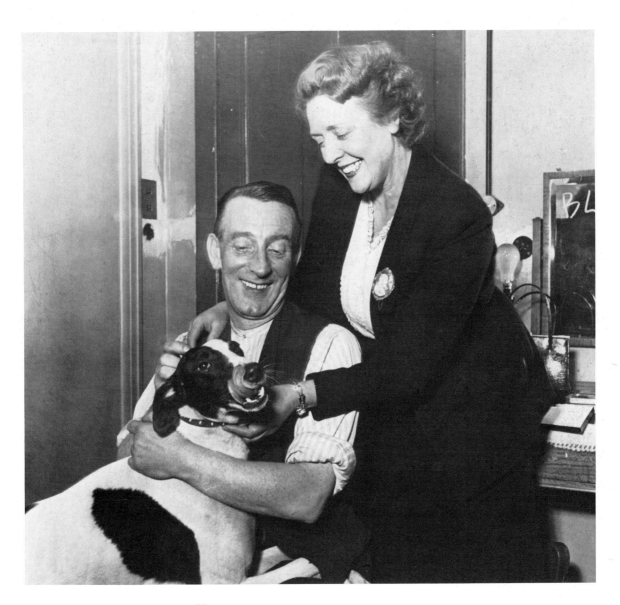

95
Wilfred and Mabel Pickles,
1953. 'Give 'im the money,
Barney' was a popular
injunction on Pickles's radio
quiz programme, 'Have A Go'.

96
Billy Graham the evangelist, in his Greater London Crusade of 1954, preached for 72 consecutive nights. A huge crowd – over 120,000 people – attended the last meeting in the rain at Wembley Stadium, including Dr Fisher, Archbishop of Canterbury, on the right of the front row.

97
'Oh, they do like to be beside the seaside' – August Bank Holiday, Blackpool Beach, 1953.

98
To the affluent worker and his family in the 1950s, holiday camps, which Billy Butlin had started in Skegness in 1937, were luxurious oases of entertainment.

99
August at Mrs Smith's boarding house, Margate, 1953. 'It happened again this month: packed trains, the beach scrums, queues for everything from donkeys to coach tours. Why do so many people insist that only an August holiday will do?'

100
August Bank Holiday, Margate Sands, 1967. In a puzzled voice, one commentator remarked that, 'People pour into Margate about lunch time on special trains and, in their ordinary clothes, go to sleep on the beach before pouring back on to the trains in late afternoon.'

101
Brighton beach, beside the
Palace Pier.

102
A quick meal in a café during a
day-trip to Dover.

103
'Chips with everything' for
those on a coach tour to Ramsgate.

104
The coconut shies, Hampstead Heath, on August Bank Holiday, 1957. It was 7.30 pm and many of the stall-holders complained, 'People don't come to the fair nowadays. They are changing their habits'.

105
A children's paradise was revealed when the tide went out at Tower Bridge, London. The youngsters were able to play in the sand dumped there in 1953 by local authorities.

106
Children play in the Gorbals,
Glasgow, 1970.

107
Marilyn Monroe with Sir
Laurence Olivier, Savoy Hotel,
15 July 1956.

108
Sir Malcolm Sargent
conducted the Last Night of the
Henry Wood Promenade
concerts in 1957. Millions
listened to these popular
concerts on radio and
television.

109
Sir John Barbirolli receives a
floral tribute on being made a
Freeman of Manchester,
22 March 1958.

110
'The Colonies Come to Town' –
the theme of the Lord Mayor's
Show, 1954. Russ Henderson
and his West Indian band seem
to leave even the walkie-talkie
policeman speechless.

BRITISH GUIANA

111
Midnight, 31 December 1962, and there's a snowstorm in London, but 10,000 people are in Trafalgar Square, some of them in the fountain, where one couple kiss the New Year in.

112
The London University students' 'Battle of Richmond' Rag is in full flow in March 1968.

113
Petticoat Lane, London,
Sunday morning 11 December
1960 – shoppers in search of the
Christmas bargain.

114
Prostitutes walked the streets
of London until the publication
of the Wolfenden Report in
1957 when they seemed to
vanish overnight. Contact was
now by means of
advertisements in newsagents'
shop windows. Typically the
cards had rounded corners
and the messages were coded
to explain the wares on offer.

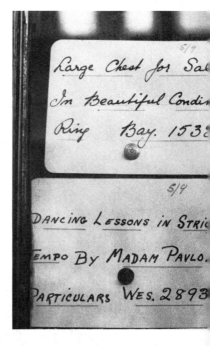

115
There were always spectators
at any time of the day or night at
strip-tease clubs in London
such as the Tropicana.

116
Buskers amuse cinema
queues, London, 1957.

117
There was more time than ever
for drinking in pubs and more
money to spend, even if the
beer never seemed as good as
it used to be.

118
As the tourist trade increased, conservation and restoration could be made to pay. After twenty years of idleness the Ffestiniog railway in Wales, which ran from Portmadoc through 27 miles of the world's finest scenery, re-opened in June 1957.

119
Stonehenge had to be protected by barbed wire from hooligans and erosion caused by too many visitors. On 21 June 1965 the Druids saw the sun rise in spectacular fashion over the Heel Stone.

120
When popular programmes
were on the radio people
listened in avidly. The Goon
Show, featuring Peter Sellers,
Spike Milligan and Harry
Secombe, was a form of
humour which left some people
unmoved but, for millions of
others, Thursday night
listening was obligatory. Here
they are recording a special
show to celebrate St David's
Day, 1956.

121
Famous among early TV
comedy programmes was
'Hancock's Half Hour', starring
Tony Hancock and Sid James,
February 1960.

122
Gilbert Harding was famous for
his rudeness and bad temper.
After a time on radio, in 'Round
Britain Quiz' and 'Twenty
Questions', he starred on
television in 'What's my Line'.
Here he is 'Face to Face' with
John Freeman in September
1960.

123

As the commentator at all the important public events, Richard Dimbleby dominated the early years of television. In May 1959 he broadcast the Council of Europe's tenth anniversary in St James's Palace, London.

124

The Irish literary tradition continued but Brendan Behan slept through the rehearsal of the play *Posterity be Damned* by his brother Dominic; beside him are his mother, father and sister-in-law. Apparently he didn't like the play for when he woke up he was sullen and angry, shouted out 'rubbish', and stalked out of the theatre.

▶ **125**
Elizabeth Taylor being carried to her plane on 27 March 1961, after leaving the London Clinic where she had been recovering from pneumonia. Standing attentively to her side is her then-husband, Eddie Fisher.

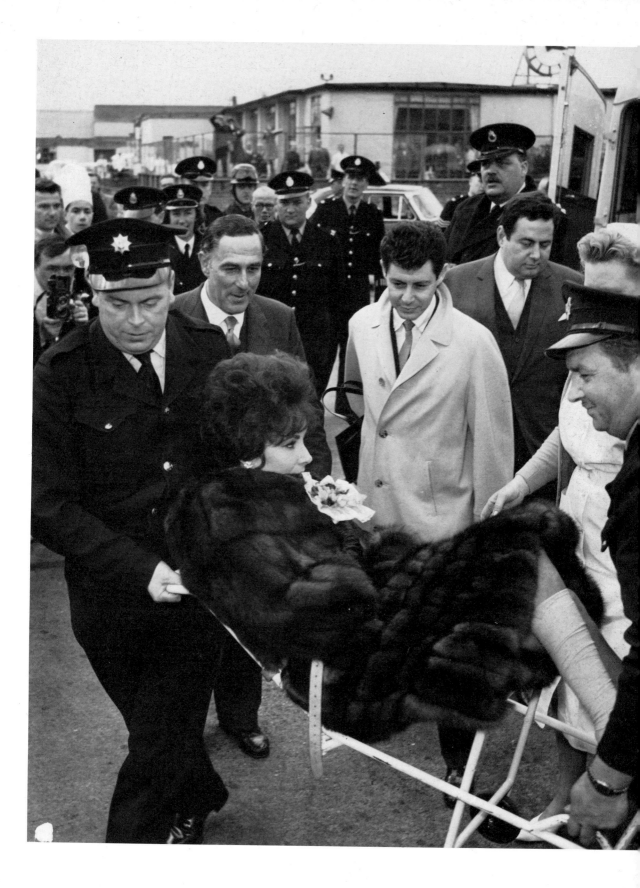

126
Foreign tours were by now
looming large in the life of
Queen Elizabeth – here she
dances the popular Ghanaian
rhythmic shuffle, 'High Life',
with Ghana's President Kwame
Nkrumah in Accra, November
1961.

127
Faces from the past – the
Commonwealth Prime
Ministers taking time off from
the July 1964 Conference. The
Queen entertains them all to
dinner at Buckingham Palace.

128
Radio Caroline broadcast pop music from a ship anchored in international waters in the North Sea. The authorities disapproved but naturally this only increased its appeal to youngsters with new-fangled transistor radios clamped to their ears.

129
The cast of the satirical TV show, 'That Was the Week That Was', at a recording studio on 7 January 1963. Among the by-now well-known faces are David Frost, Millicent Martin, Lance Percival and Roy Kinnear.

130
In the 1950s distinctively British films came into fashion such as *The Ladykillers* with Alec Guinness, Peter Sellers, Herbert Lom, Danny Green and Cecil Parker.

131
Later British films only made a
lot of money if aimed at an
international market. The Bond
films, based on Ian Fleming's
thrillers, were huge successes.
Sean Connery and Gert Frobe
starred in *Goldfinger*.

132
A reflection of the public
desire for entertainment as
well as news in the morning
papers was the publication of
the *Sun* in 1964, the first
mass-circulation daily paper
since 1930. Here the *Sun*'s
editorial chief, Hugh Cudlipp,
looks at proof copies (perhaps
even page 3) of the first
edition of the new paper in
the machine room on
15 September 1964.

133
Foyles, the world's largest bookshop in Charing Cross Road, London, held literary lunches for authors which were often in the news. Two of the world's richest men, Nubar Gulbenkian (left) and J. Paul Getty, came face to face, or even closer, in March 1965.

134
In a country yearning for novelty, Dr Barbara Moore aroused intense national interest when she walked from Edinburgh to London in December 1959.

135–140

If it had a gimmick, it would hit
the headlines. **135**: Stanley
Tozer on his 'Jockey Ball'.
136: actors dressed as city gents
to advertise a restaurant.
137: the Butlin Marathon walk
from John O'Groats to Land's End.
138: the hula hoop.
139: full-frontal in Trafalgar Square.
140: the leaping milkman of
Hamworthy, Dorset.

141
Tennis at Wimbledon was an
ideal television sport. In 1961,
in the first all-British Women's
Singles final since 1914, Angela
Mortimer (shown here)
defeated Christine Truman.

142
Jim Laker at Old Trafford in
1956 having taken nine wickets
in the first Australian innings of
the Test Match. With all ten
wickets as well in the second
innings, Laker set an
astonishing cricket record that
is unlikely to be equalled.

143
Crowds of West Indies
supporters swarm onto the
pitch at Lord's to congratulate
their heroes. Colin Cowdrey,
injured arm and all, had just
held them to a draw on the final
day of the second Test Match, 1963.

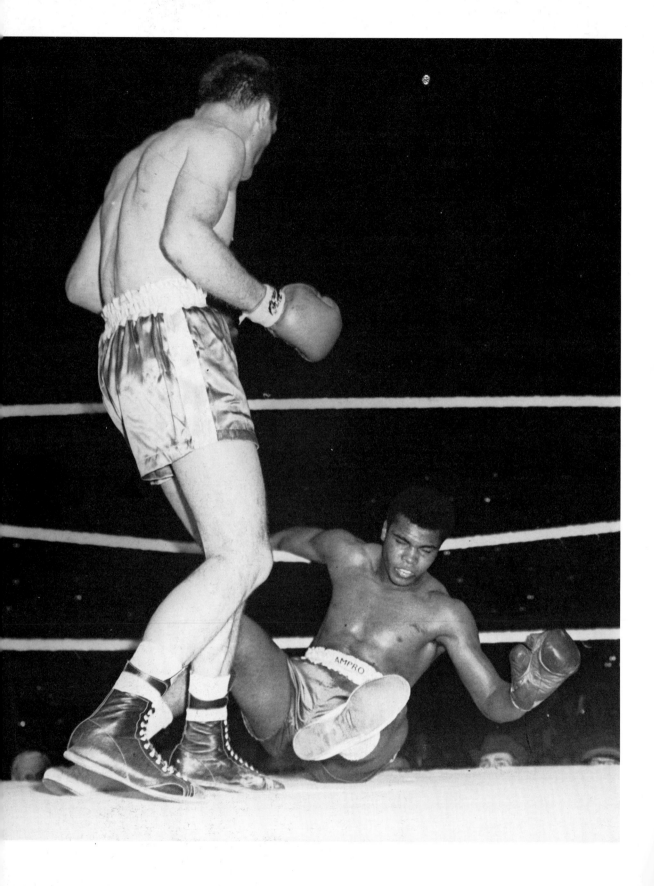

◄ 144
Cassius Clay, later Muhammad Ali, dominated the boxing rings of the world – except for one moment in June 1963 when Henry Cooper, British and Empire Heavyweight Champion, put 'the Greatest' on the floor. Clay, however, went on to win the fight.

► 145
Long-jumper Lynn Davies, gold medal-winner at the Tokyo Olympics in 1964, relaxes at an hotel near London Airport before going to meet the Queen.

► 146
An enthusiastic supporter rushes onto the field at the Cup Final in 1966 after the hero of the match, Mike Trebilcock, had scored Everton's second goal. As police remove the supporter, Everton captain Brian Labone remonstrates with him, while Brian Harris tries on the police officer's hat for size.

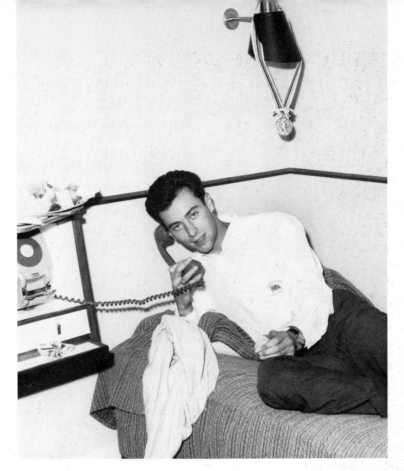

147
A month before his death in
January 1967, Donald
Campbell tries out an
amphibious scooter.

148
In 1968 South Africa refused to
allow the MCC to take on tour
the Cape Coloured player Basil
D'Oliveira. 'Dolly' signs
autographs for young fans
having already heard that the
tour was off. South Africa from
this time on was to be largely
ostracized from international
sport.

149
Tony Jacklin playing in 1968. In 1969 he raised the nation's temperature by winning the British Open Championship, and again in 1970 the US Open Championship.

150

Easy come, easy go – a racing
tipster in 1958, prepared to
take bids for all sorts of sports.

Never So Good?

151
As Minister for Housing, Harold Macmillan organized a housing drive to fulfil Conservative election pledges. On 16 June 1954 he opened an exhibition aimed at encouraging local authorities to make new houses from old. Two terrace houses were to be converted into three flats.

152
Harold Macmillan's famous
remark that the British people
'had never had it so good' was
borrowed from the US
Democrats who had used it in
1952. Whether or not it was true
of Britain, Macmillan himself–
here at the Earl of Swinton's
'Glorious Twelfth' grouse
shooting, 1964– had
considerable style.

153

The road to a gold-plated Daimler might after all be through a win on the pools, and enormous sums were wagered every week. Lady Docker is assisted by her cook, Mrs L. Goodium, in the task of filling in her football pool coupon.

154

In 1960 schooling at Harrow cost £462 a year. Harrow headmaster, Dr R. L. James, calls the roll as the boys file past tipping their boaters.

155
It was an age of 'topside' said
J. B. Priestley. Top people read
The Times but with a boom on
in the City in 1960, the *Financial
Times* was more interesting.

156
Periods of boom alternated
with depression – it came to be
called the stop-go economy.
This is the floor of the old
London Stock Exchange on 30
May 1962, the day after shares
had had their worst fall for
more than thirty years. (Note
the exchange rate of $2.80
which now seems like a mirage.)

157

When seven coal pits were
closed in 1959 the Welsh
miners came to London to
lobby their MPs. 'Let us give
the coal to OAPs' they said, and
old-age pensioners who had
been urged to keep warm with
hot-water bottles agreed.

158
An old crofter in Lewis in the
Outer Hebrides had little to
show for the 1960 boom.

159

'Three youngsters skipping in
the sunlight – the address is
Lamb Cliff, Stone. A street
which lies in the very shadow
of a cement factory, where
rooftops, walls and gardens are
literally caked with a coating of
cement dust – a picture which
prompts the questions "How
many more generations before
we solve the problem of
pollution in North-West Kent".'

160
Down and out in South Kensington, 1968.

161
Meals out in cafés for the homeless,
1965.

162
Frenzied search for bargains at
the Old Salt Market, the Gorbals,
Glasgow, 1970.

▲ **163**
In 1954, more than twelve years after the Blitz, rebuilding around St Paul's, London, is just beginning. In the immediate foreground would be Watling House, a block of offices, and behind on the left more offices (Gateway House). Running from right foreground to St Paul's is Watling Street. On the right of this can be seen steelwork for new offices of the Bank of England.

◀ **164**
Scaffolding was put round the dome of St Paul's in 1965 to repair damage caused during the Blitz.

▶ **165**
On the back of the shopping boom, Selfridges in Oxford Street, London, had a splendid face-lift in 1957.

GRIGGS & SON
LIMITED

SGB SGB
SGB SGB
SGB SGB
SGB

166
A general view of the Elephant and Castle Redevelopment Scheme, 1958.

167
Symbolizing the way that the building boom ripped the hearts out of many old towns – sometimes successfully, though often not – new flats arise from central Dundee, with the Firth of Tay in the background, in 1966.

168
Power overshadows paddlers at Rugeley, Staffordshire. The cooling tower on the left was, in July 1966, the largest in the world.

169
In 1967 Dungeness Nuclear Power Station was planned as the largest such station in the world. The two reactors – No 1 the more advanced in construction – are seen here from the top of a 400-ton Goliath crane. In the background are the old and new lighthouses.

170
Compulsory purchase orders
were the prerogative of local
councils with brand-new
development schemes in mind.
Mr Clark, a £9 13s. 6d. a week
painter, and his family, camp
on the pavement after being
evicted by Finchley Council
under a compulsory purchase
order in 1957.

171

A compulsory purchase order in 1968 on Victoria Road, Leytonstone, home and business of former prisoner-of-war Steve Hurn, was stoutly resisted. 'I have built up my motor business', said Mr Hurn, 'and it is my whole life. The house is now really smart as I have put a lot of work into it. Both Joan and I are prepared to defend our home to the end.' Their efforts, alas, were brave but unsuccessful.

172
'LCC Matchboxes' said the
contemporary by-line
contemptuously on 16 October
1963. Updated pre-fabs
erected near the West India
Docks to help with the problem
of London's homeless.

173
Woman magazine surveyed a
brighter habitat for two
bachelor girls in 1959.

174
Wine and Spirits Department,
Harrods, London, 1954.

175
Shopping in a new self-service
supermarket, February 1965.
When Retail Price
Maintenance was removed,
Anthony Jackson Foodfare
supermarket, Acton, slashed
whisky by seven shillings a
bottle. The check-out girl has a
nicely fashionable beehive
hair-do.

176
One satisfied London customer
at the December sales in 1956.
Mr Smith of St John's Hill,
Battersea, queued overnight
for one of four TV sets knocked
down to £1 a time.

177
One way of carrying the
shopping home.

178
Bessie Braddock, MP, plus
teddy bear, after opening the
new reception centre of Bear
Brand Hosiery, Liverpool,
October 1962.

179
Ernest Marples, Minister of
Transport, orchestrated the
motorway building boom. He
brought a welcome element of
light-heartedness onto the
political scene.

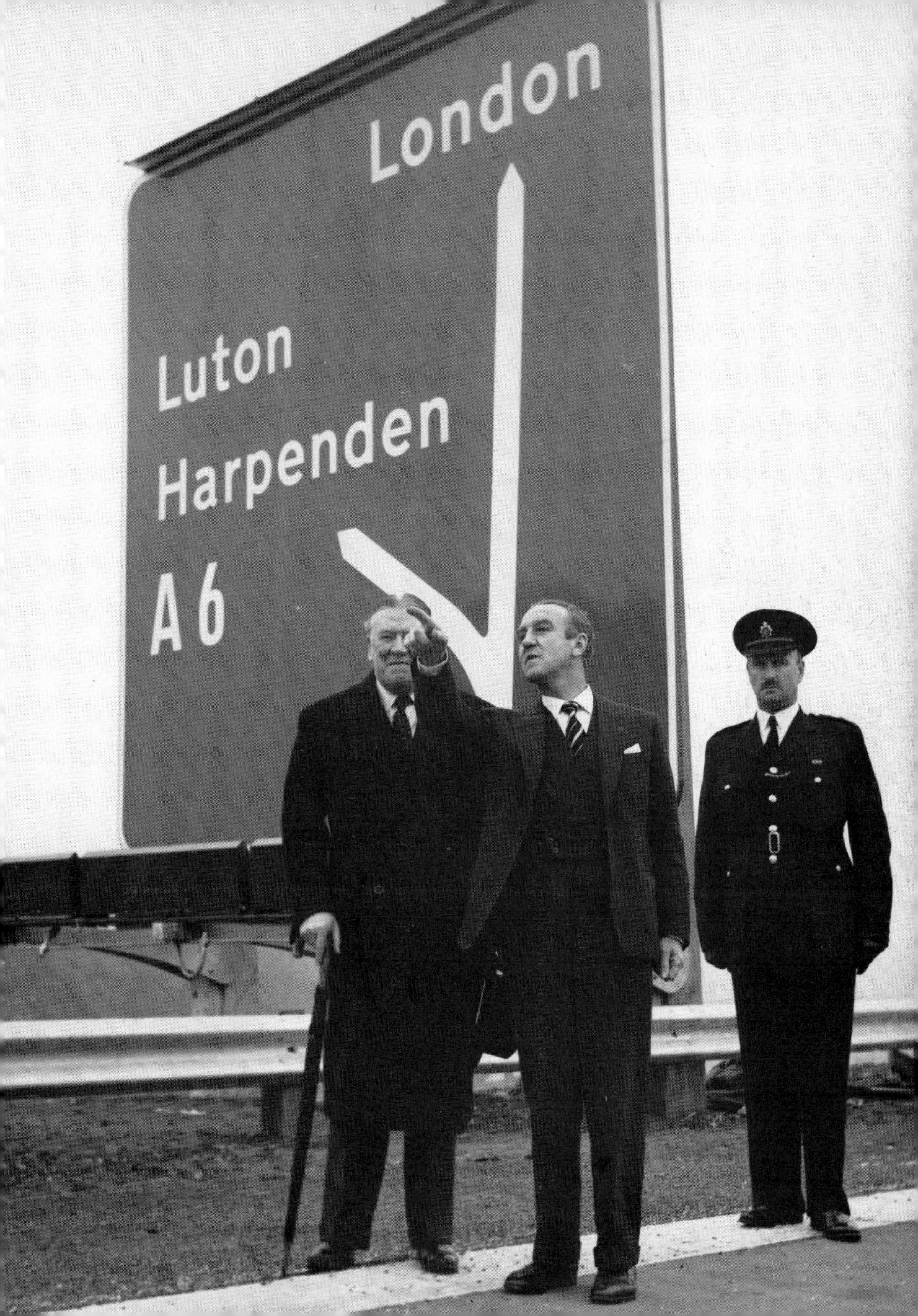
London
Luton
Harpenden
A6

180
Cars were in great demand, but the huge stockpile here, outside Ford's Halewood factory, was unplanned. Assembly men were about to begin a four-day week caused by a strike of car delivery men, August 1965.

181
New buildings and plant were erected at a cost of well over £10,000,000 for the production of the new car announced on 26 August 1959 as the Austin Seven and Morris Mini Minor. The price was £350, plus purchase tax in Britain of £146 19s. 2d. Fuel consumption was 50 mpg. Workers rub down a line of car bodies before they receive the finishing coat of paint.

182
While the steam train trundles across the Forth Bridge, Scotland, in July 1953, a new toll bridge over the river for road traffic was being discussed in the House of Commons.

183
On 8 September 1964 Scotland's biggest-ever traffic jam piled up for twenty-five miles both sides of the Forth Bridge. A flow of between 5000 and 6000 cars taxed bridge staff to exhaustion point.

184
Valuing its serenity, the village
of Beer in Devon refused to
admit cars during the summer;
so the car park outside the
village was as good a place as
any to picnic.

185
The motoring organizations
grew enormously. The price of
membership was little
compared to the help they
could give in an emergency.

186

The theme of the Lord Mayor's
Show in November 1964 was
'Motoring through the Ages'.
The sports cars included: front
row, Lotus Elan (left) and
Triumph Spitfire 4; second
row, Sunbeam Tiger (left) and
an MGB.; third row, Austin
Healey 3000 (left) and an AC
Cobra; back row, Daimler Dart
(left) and XKE Jaguar. Behind
on the float are a Rover T. 4
turbine and Minis. 'The roar of
an exhaust is a modern mating
call', said one authority
emphatically.

187

At the Elephant and Castle,
bicycles and motorbikes were
brought into use again when
the London bus drivers were
on strike in 1958.

188

Among new forms of transport Britain led the world with Christopher Cockerell's invention, the hovercraft. An early hovercraft at Ramsgate in the 1960s takes local people on a pleasure trip.

189

Those who argued that the Channel Tunnel would increase the prosperity of the south-east found themselves up against those who feared that it would destroy the natural habitats of the area and increase local pollution. This is Shakespeare Hole, the site of the nineteenth-century attempt, in 1970 just before closure.

190

In central London, Centre Point was built. During the boom years it was said that it paid to keep it empty as its value with vacant possession rose uninterruptedly, no rates being levied on empty buildings.

191
The giant domes at
Fylingdales, Yorkshire, under
construction in 1962 as part of
the Ballistic Missile Early
Warning System.

Yesterday's Children

192
Yesterday's children at school
were taller, heavier and
healthier – and in the postwar
baby boom, more numerous –
than any previous generation.

193
Winkle-picker shoes and
drain-pipe trousers were part
of the new uniform. 'Noddy'
Carne, 19, Ronald Hill, 19, John
Brown, 17, David Turner, 17,
just standing on the corner
watching the girls go by.

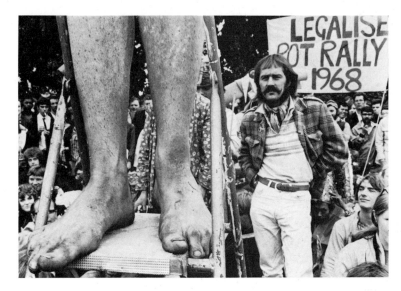

198
An American psychiatrist
organized a 5000-strong LEMAR
(Legalize marajuana) rally in
Hyde Park in 1968.

199
Hair style was an important distinguishing badge between the groups of yesterday's children, but almost any cut would do as long as it was sufficiently outrageous. A fine 'Afro' head of hair at the LEMAR rally, 1968.

200
The respectability which the clean image of the Beatles had earned for pop music was lost when groups and their followers used drugs, particularly 'pot' (marajuana). Two members of the Rolling Stones came to court in May 1967 whilst their supporters in the crowd outside the courtroom called for the legalization of marajuana.

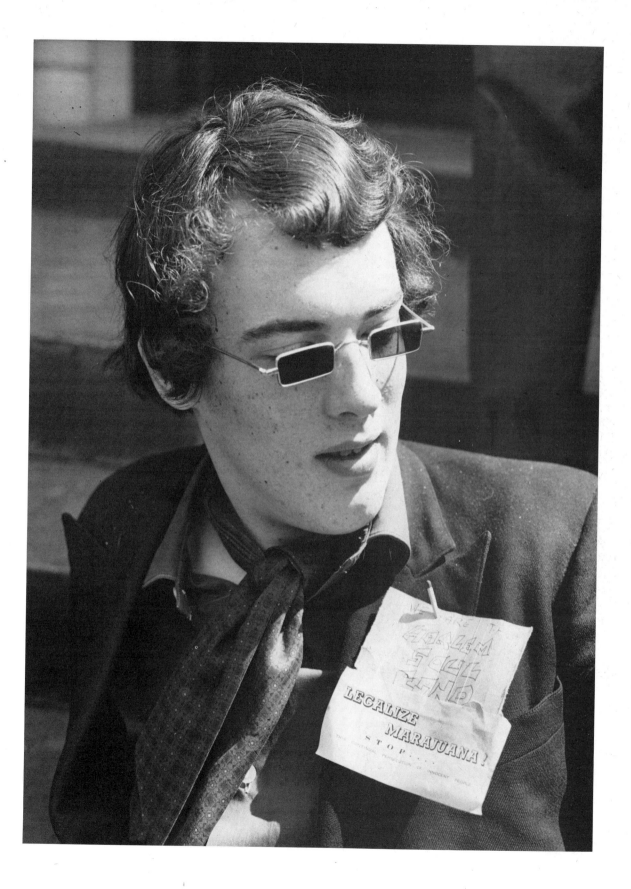

201
In the King's Road, Chelsea,
the uncertainties show through.

202
The girl 'beatnik' is bare-footed, probably not from poverty but because it was believed that shoes insulated the body from life-forces which could only be gained through direct contact with mother earth.

203
Big Daddy Zoots Warren's
beatnik pad in Scotland.
Blankets were hung over
windows to stop people
looking in.

204
Fifteen beatniks lived in a
house in Gambier Terrace,
Liverpool, 1960, but soon after
this picture was taken they
were evicted for burning the
furniture for fuel.

◀ **205**
Anything goes – the casual
style in Regent Street, 1969.

▲ **206**
The scene in Sam Widges'
coffee bar, Berwick Street,
Soho. Coffee bars were an
important meeting place,
where adults would feel
strangers and one cup of coffee
could last a whole evening.

207
Schoolchildren in Dreamland,
Margate – in the background
a pin-ball machine
appropriately called
'Teacher's Pet'.

208
Cigarettes, alcohol and hairdos
all speak of affluence in a late
1960s pub.

209
Convinced that the
establishment press reported
their activities unfavourably or
ignored them completely,
teenagers welcomed an
underground press. Such
papers as *IT* (International
Times) were sold on the street
or in cafés. An 'underground'
news-seller in Oxford Street
sells a copy of *IT* to an
American tourist. Much of the
underground press soon ran
out of money or the printers
took fright and refused to print.

210
Australian Richard Neville,
editor of *Ink* and *Oz*, who was
prosecuted for obscenity in the
notorious 'school-kids issue' of
Oz. On the wall is a poster for
Release, an organization
concerned with drugs.

211

The *Black Dwarf*, another
publication of the underground
press, was edited by Tariq Ali
and concerned itself with
student revolution and power,
although the placard wearer at
the LSE sit-in thinks that 'the
only true goal of a revolution is
the pursuit of unlicensed
pleasure'.

212

Hari Krishna disciples, playing drums and tambourines, were common sights in Oxford Street, but in August 1970 they went to Margate where, the photographer recalls, 'They chanted a mantra for peace in answer to the violence of the skinheads' rave-up. It seemed to work because they were joined by the skinheads in a half-mile queue which snaked up and down the sea front all afternoon, all of them chanting in unison'.

213
Teenage violence in Clacton,
Easter 1964, led to 127 arrests, a
purple heart pep-pill search by
the police, and police vetting of
this scooter invasion the
following weekend.

214
In a less authoritarian world,
there was a violent side to the
teenage cult of enjoyment.
Mods and rockers often fought
against each other, particularly
on Bank Holidays. The
policeman on the right holds a
black-sheathed knife, having
broken up hostilities between
rival gangs at Hastings 1964.

215
Defiant to the last. Policemen in
fetching white helmets drag
away a youth on Brighton
beach, May 1964, following
clashes between mods and
rockers.

216
The skinhead look.

Demo

217
Sir Oswald Mosley addresses
the faithful in his Union
Movement, a survivor from
pre-war days, on 10 February
1954, at the Wilmot Street
School, Bethnal Green Road,
London. Subject: Europe
against communism.

218
The Campaign for Nuclear
Disarmament (CND) attracted
considerable public attention
(and often over 100,000
marchers) by its annual Easter
march from the Nuclear
Research Establishment at
Aldermaston to London. The
first march was in 1958. Here, in
1960, Canon John Collins and
Mr Michael Foot lead the way.

Text in image: THE WEEKLY PEACE NEWSPAPER / H. BOMB PROTEST MARCH / PEACE NEWS / EVERY 6 FRIDAY

219
The sleep of the just on the Aldermaston march.

220
Bertrand Russell at the 1961 march. 'This idea of weapons of mass destruction' he said 'is utterly horrible . . . I will not pretend to obey a government which is organizing a massacre of mankind.'

221
There were other demonstrations for peace. One such march moved from Trafalgar Square to the American Embassy in November 1960.

222
Speakers' Corner, Hyde Park, provided a more traditional platform for protests.

223
Police reinforcements were
rushed to London's Notting Hill
Gate on 1 September 1958 as
race riots broke out for the
second time in twenty-four
hours. The riots began after
gangs of white youths had
jeered at coloured people.

224
Apprentices tour Sheffield in
1960 in a reasonably
good-mannered demand for
more money. With the advent
of television, protests would
soon become a great deal
more visible and more violent.

225

The credit squeeze in 1960 was blamed for redundancies in the car industry and workers demonstrated outside Earls Court at the opening of the Motor Show on 19 October 1960. Work-sharing and the right to work were slogans which were to become increasingly popular.

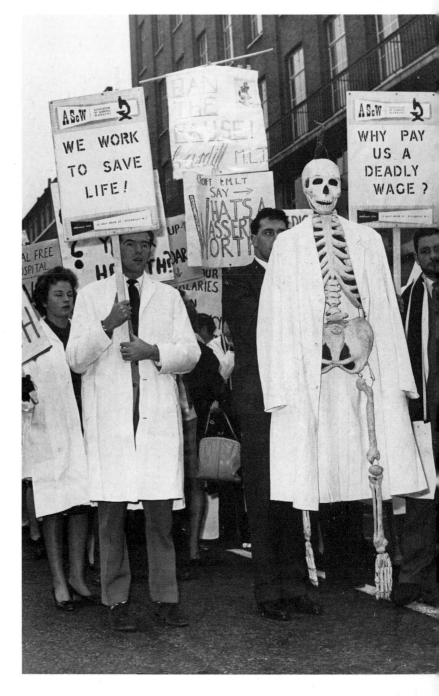

226
Villagers of Swanley, Kent,
demonstrate in favour of a
zebra crossing and by-pass,
July 1960.

227
Medical laboratory technicians
in London in 1961 demand
better pay.

The signs in the image read:

DONT BE BEASTLY
MR BEVINS

STREET
TORY
TO, BEAUT.
.HAND.
OF. MORE

ANNUAL.
LEAVE.

NT.DILL]
ONG.THE
T. MAR
ALON
FOR. A WEEK
WITH.
PAY

CIVIL SERVANT
IN
NAME ONLY.
GIVE US CIVIL
SERVICE
LEAVE.
SAY LONDON FACTORIES

MEN GET
DOUBLE LEAVE
FOR 'REST &
LEISURE'
WHO SAYS WOMEN
ARE THE
WEAKER SEX?

PRODUCTION
UP!

OUR
SPIRITS
DOWN
AISE THEM WITH
CREASED LEAVE

ENFIELD
FACTORY

HOLLOWAY
FACTORY

OUR
SPIRITS
DOWN
THEM WITH
ANNUAL LEAVE

UNFAIR to
All T.M's.

MORE ANNUAL
LEAVE

POEU

P.M.G.
IF YOU WANT
SERVANT
IN CIVI

228
Women post-office workers
demonstrate outside the Pier
Ballroom, Hastings, Sussex,
where 500 members of the Post
Office Engineering Union were
holding their 1962 annual
conference. The women
wanted equal holidays with
their male colleagues.

229
In October 1963, neo-Nazi
leader Colin Jordan, head of
Britain's National Socialist
Party, married the niece of
fashion designer Christian
Dior. After giving the Nazi
salute on arriving at the party's
headquarters in Notting Hill
Gate the couple cut their ring
fingers, and mingled the blood
on to a copy of *Mein Kampf*.

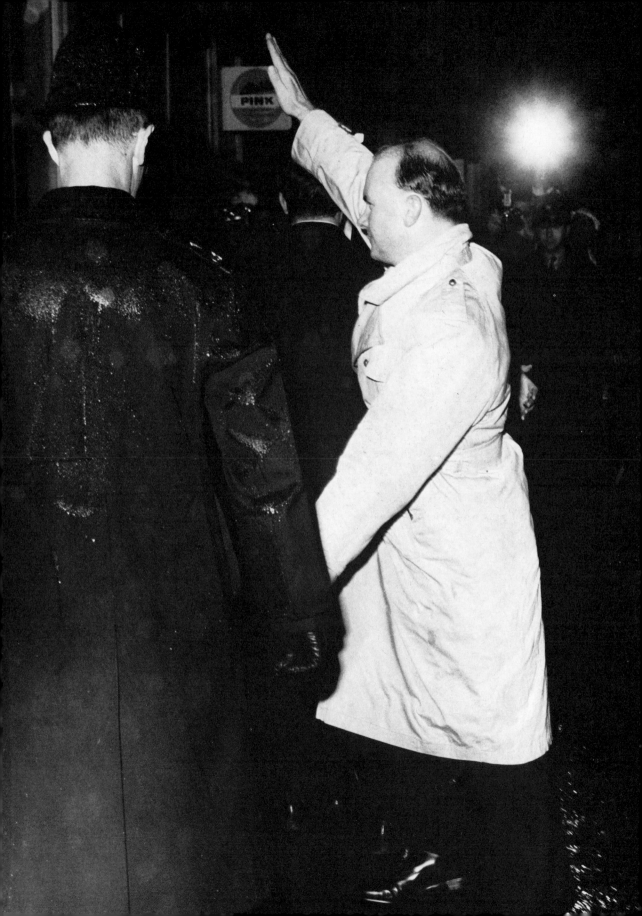

230
In the early 1960s, Martin
Webster, who subsequently
became a leader of the
National Front, was its press
officer and could be seen in
snack bars in Earls Court,
London, talking to followers.
His hair is slicked back in a DA
(Duck's Arse) cut. From a small
stand in the street opposite
Earls Court Station, he and
others proclaimed against 'the
filthy slime of beatniks
sweeping across the land'.

231
The Chinese cultural
revolution created great
excitement outside the
Chinese Legation in London on
29 August 1967.

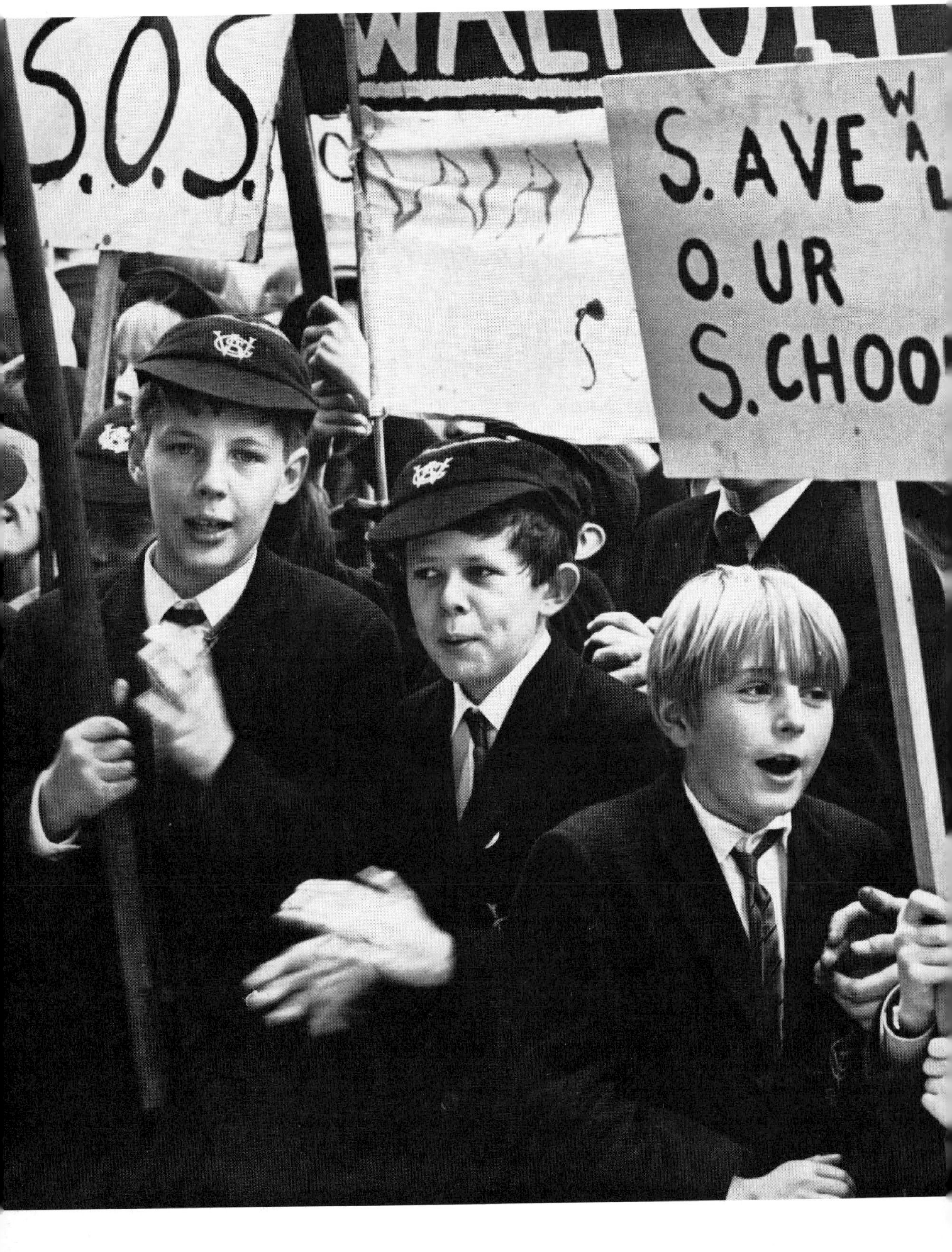
S.O.S.
S.AVE
O.UR
S.CHOO

232
Even young schoolboys got in
on the act – boys from Walpole
Grammar School, Ealing,
demonstrate against a
proposed school merger in
1968.

233
Grosvenor Square, 1968. The
'Women in Black' silent protest march
pass the American Embassy.

234
The boot goes in as thousands of students take part in the famous anti-Vietnam war demonstration march in London on 27 October 1968. Violence broke out near the American Embassy in Grosvenor Square.

235
'Who is Enoch Powell' declares the poster – his prophecies of forthcoming racial conflict were the subject of several demonstrations, including one at Birmingham University in June 1968.

236
Hyde Park, January 1969 – over 90,000 postal workers were on strike in favour of a pay-claim by overseas telegraphists.

237
Welsh Society students demonstrate in 1969 against a visit by the Prince of Wales to Aberystwyth, where Prince Charles was to have a university term. On the roof-top, out of harm's way, are loyalist students.

238
Northern Ireland supporters
of Ian Paisley demonstrated
outside St Paul's when the
leader of Britain's Roman
Catholics, Cardinal Heenan,
spoke in a unity service in
January 1969.

239
The beginning of the present
Troubles in Northern Ireland –
the Shankhill Road, Belfast,
August 1969.

240
Bernadette Devlin, at 22 the
youngest MP, demonstrated
with London workers in a 1969
May Day protest against the
government White Paper, 'In
Place of Strife', an attempt to
remodel union law.

241
Demonstration of a peaceful
sort – but the Back Britain
Campaign caught the public
imagination for only a short
time before fizzling out.

Hard at Work

242
The *Owl* trawling in the North
Sea, October 1953.

243
Coping with snow in
Newcastle, January 1955.

244
A 'nippy' waitress in one of the
Joe Lyons cafés.

245
Cleaners at work in the Stock
Exchange at the end of a day's
trading, 1953.

246
Behind the scenes at the Royal
Academy, 1953. From the top of
the main staircase looking
down to the front entrance of
the Academy the four 'Mrs
Mopps' kept this fine old
building clean and polished.

247
After fourteen years of
government restriction the
London Corn Exchange was
allowed to operate as a free
market in 1953. Hands
containing grain are held out
for inspection. Much of the
business was conducted
outside in the streets in the light
of day.

248
Christmas turkey auction,
Smithfield Market, London,
December 1953.

249
Knife-grinder, Nelson Smith, at
work in New Eltham, May 1961.

250
Former nurse, Kay Thorburn,
who took a Ministry of
Agriculture rat-catching
course, was Britain's only
full-time 'pestologist'. Here, in
February 1960, she is
destroying rats on a Middlesex
farm.

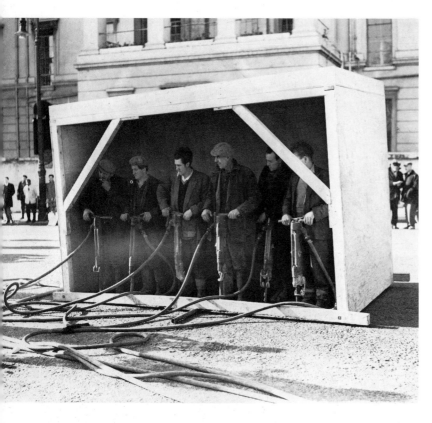

251
Six road-workers take part in
noise abatement tests with
automatic road drills in a
sound-proof box outside St
George's Hospital, London,
February 1961.

252
The tunnel under the Tyne,
5500 feet long, 31 feet in
diameter, November 1963.

253
Nelson had a facial from a steeplejack in Trafalgar Square, February 1963.

254
Work went on all night at the old Covent Garden (before it moved in the 1970s to a purpose-built Hall across the Thames), and the porters' little carts were a principal method of loading and unloading fruit and vegetables.

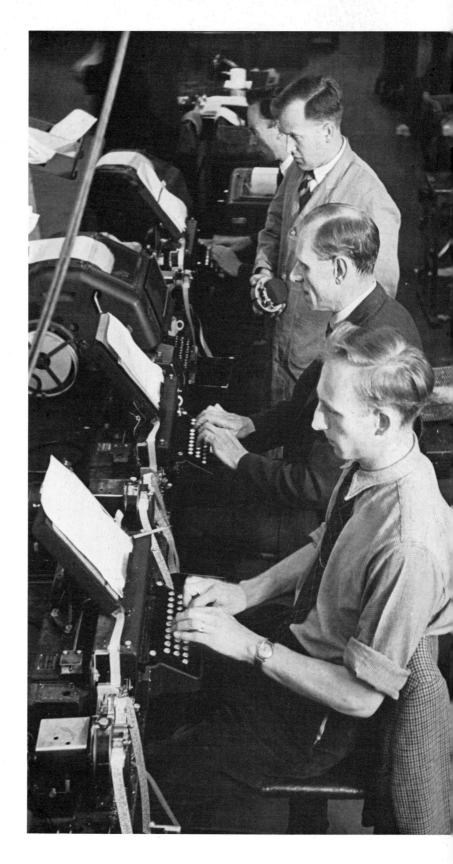

255
In the East End of London the
sweat shops of the rag trade
employed a third of the local
population on garment process
work.

256
In Reuters' news agency, lines
of operators typed the news
which went simultaneously to
London and provincial
newspapers and on teleprinter
to Reuter offices throughout the
world.

257
Prior to a wool auction, a
shipment is inspected at
Colonial and Eagle wharves,
London, 15 May 1958.

258
The 'waste-not-want-not' town,
Dewsbury, Yorkshire, the
centre of the waste rag trade.
Fred Booth looks at the shoddy
from which wool felts and
mattress fillings are made, 1953.

259
Although eighty-five-year-old
Jacob Playfoot had retired from
the cricket-ball factory at
Hildenborough, Kent, he
continued at home as a 'closer'
– one who stitches the leather
pieces together.

260
At Dinorwic Quarry, near
Caernarvon, Welsh slate for
the roofs of Nos 10, 11 and 12
Downing Street is brought in
for processing, 1962.

261
Housed partly in tunnels that
were originally dug for a
proposed underground
railway, the Kingsway Trunk
Exchange in 1968 could handle
2,000,000 telephone calls a
week. These moles working
100 feet underground must
surely have welcomed
automation.

262
An early computer in Birkbeck
College, London, 1962, used by
the Department of Numerical
Automation for linguistic
analysis.

263
Ever hopeful ballad-sheet
seller. 'All my own work' was to
become an increasingly
plaintive note as the white-hot
technological age dawned.

Country Matters

264
Winter Hirings, Carlisle, 21 November 1951. Tradition and old ways died hard and life on the land was resistant to change, but the period was to see the end of intensive cultivation by many farm labourers as the machine took over and fewer people were needed. In Carlisle, the farm worker traditionally sought the highest price for his labour at the spring and winter hirings. The bargain was sealed with half-a-crown and everybody retired to the fair. But it was a dying custom and at this winter hiring only twenty-five bargains were struck.

265
Tea break for apple pickers at
Scadbury Farm near Sidcup,
Kent, August 1950. Beauty of
Bath was the early fruiting
variety. The man on the left
drinks cold tea from a bottle.

266
Cutting brussel sprout tops,
December 1958. Forty-three of
Miss Crew's fifty-seven years
had been spent on the land.

267
Crofter awaiting his turn at the
cattle sale, Tarbert, Isle of
Harris, Outer Hebrides,
October 1960.

268
The population of the
Hebridean island of Soay fell
from 150 at the start of the
century to 27 in 1953. Sandy
Campbell, the last islander to
go, packs his pipes to leave.

269
Peggy McLeod makes butter
by hand on her croft in South
Uist, Outer Hebrides,
September 1961.

270

Shetland peat solves the fuel problem but there is no easy way – the peats must all be cut, turned, dried and carted by hand. Mrs Malcolmson of Quarff carrying her peat in a 'keshie', August 1957.

271

A Welsh shepherd brings in a lame sheep from the winter snows of his hill farm, Llangaver, North Wales.

272
One of the cockle ladies of Penclawdd, South Wales, Mrs Lizzie Davies had worked on the sands for most of her life, though she was only fifty years old.

273
At the monthly cattle market in an Irish village the boy is employed to keep the cattle away from the door.

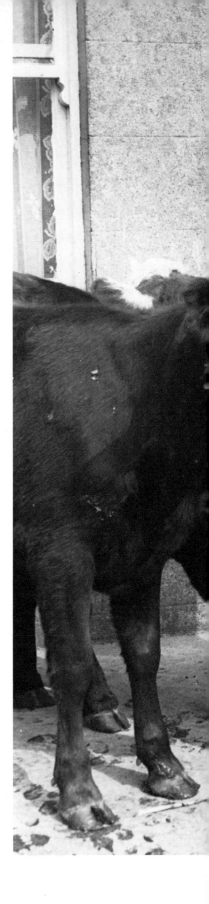

274
Eighty-five-year-old John
Taylor makes hay at Tarleton,
Lancashire, October 1956.

275
In 1954, eighty-year-old
Florence Allbeury, a Kent
fruit-picker, still worked
forty-seven hours a week, and
cycled ten miles each day. In
the words of the foreman 'she is
the best fruit worker I've had,
man or woman'.

276
Making his last delivery by
yoke and pail is Mr Reginald
Warren in the village of
Thorncombe, Dorset, one of
the few remaining areas where
it was not yet compulsory for
milk to be sold in capped
bottles, 6 July 1962.

277
There were not many stilt
workers left in the hop fields of
Kent by the 1950s, for the
system of hop stringing had
changed with the times.
But at Hermitage Farm,
Wateringbury, Mr George
Marden still preferred to use
the traditional method.

278
Mrs Mary Wright, 64 (left), and
her sister Mrs Alice Smith, 68,
at work in the hop gardens at
Paddock Wood, Kent, in 1958.
They used to come down
regularly from Millwall,
London.

279
Typical of the Women's
Institute throughout the country
in 1953 – the ladies of Birling,
Kent, with a basket-work
session in progress.

280
Afternoon post delivery to a
shop in Dunster, Somerset,
April 1956.

281
Hard work pushing a seed
barrow up and down a
twenty-acre field. A one-year
ley was being undersown on
winter wheat at Tithe Barn
Farm, Send, Surrey, May 1956.

282
East Malling Research Centre
adapts a sprayer for nursery
work, 1951. The high wheels
enabled it to straddle several
rows.

283
Britain's loneliest island – Fair Isle – where tractors of the small, handy type were the best form of transport in July 1957.

284
A combine harvester at work on barley in 1957. It seemed enormous then but it was a toy compared to the machines which were to follow.

285

Farmers' Co-operative, Vale of Penllyn,
Wales, 19 May 1951. Under the
direction of E. B. Owen, manager
and salesman combined, the venture
flourished. Notice the warning
sign on the counter – an
indication of the increasing role
chemicals were playing in
agricultural life.

286

Foot-and-mouth disease, with
compulsory slaughter of
infected animals, was
heart-breaking for farmers
who saw their herds wiped out.
Disinfection was one method of
control and a barrier of straw
bales closes the road to the
Crickley Barrow, November 1967.

287
Motorway development often
gobbled up rich farmland,
splitting farms in half. Giant
excavators bite into the chalk to
carve out the foundations for a
viaduct which would carry the
new M2 motorway 800 feet
across the Stockbury Valley
south-west of Sittingbourne,
Kent, June 1962.

288

Heavier lorries would fast break up road surfaces and make old bridges obsolete. Through Eynsford in Kent these lorries carried spring wheat seed destined for France to make up for a disastrous French harvest in 1961.

289
With the loss of many
traditional seasonal jobs the
gypsies were less welcome on
the farm. Their attractive
caravans were being replaced
by motorized ones like these,
which had been towed to the
grass verge on the A2.

290
Saturday morning by the Toll
Board of the Ashford Cattle
Market, 1970, where not only
cattle were sold.

291
Clergy, choir and parishioners
of Aylesford, Kent, bless the
crops and fields of Hermitage
Farm, Barming, on the evening
of Ascension Day, 30 May 1960.

Remembrances

292
The last train in England to
have a man walk in front with a
red flag – Dover in the 1950s.

293
The Cold War created great
interest in espionage and the
most notorious case of the 1950s
– still in the news today – was
that of the defectors Burgess
and Maclean. Here, Kim
Philby, former First Secretary
at the British Embassy in
Washington, and named by
Foreign Minister Harold
Macmillan in Parliament in
connection with the missing
British diplomats Burgess and
Maclean, gives a press
conference in Kensington on 8
November 1955. Philby himself
fled to Russia in 1963.

294
The tall hat of Archbishop
Makarios was a regular image
on the screens and in the
newspapers of the mid-1950s.
Here the Archbishop, the
voluble mouthpiece of Enosis,
the union with Greece
movement, is photographed in
London on his way to the
United Nations in 1954.

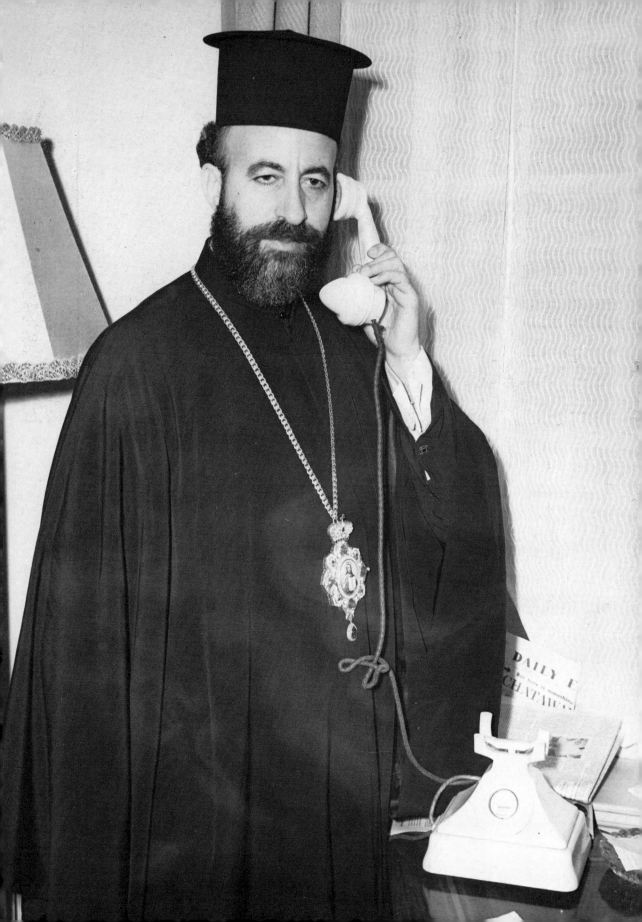

295
Sir Anthony Eden, the Prime Minister, speaks to the nation on television about the Suez crisis on 8 August 1956.

296
Pictures from Port Said. Corporal John Grimwood of Walworth, London, digs in on the bank of the Suez Canal at El Cap station on the road to Ismailia, 12 November 1956.

297

British listeners heard the
regular 'cheep...cheep...
cheep' of a Russian satellite on
their radios every 90 minutes
when the satellite was in their
half of the world. Mr Griffiths
and Mr Pearson relay it at the
BBC receiving and
measurement station at
Tatsfield, Kent, 6 October 1957.

298

On 6 February 1958 a BEA
plane crashed at Munich with
the Manchester United football
team on board, on their way
back from Belgrade. Seven of
the team were killed, the rest,
like Matt Busby and Bobby
Charlton, miraculously
survived. It was a disaster
which stunned not just football
supporters but the whole
nation.

299
The winter of 1962–3 stands as
one of the hardest in memory,
not just for the snow but for the
fog – 'smog' in the big cities –
which blanketed much of the
country and claimed the lives
of over 40 people in London
alone.

300
Graham Sutherland's 70-foot
tapestry, 'Christ in Majesty',
enters Coventry Cathedral in
March 1962.

301
The big freeze of 1963
immobilized most shipping
activity in Whitstable harbour
but the cargo vessel
Resurgence (right) managed to
cheat the weather, and is being
unloaded. Pack ice extended
for more than a quarter of a
mile from the harbour and
entrance.

302
The 1964 Olympic gold
medallist, Ann Packer,
'chaired' by members of her
home village, Moulsford in
Berkshire.

303
William John Vassall, a
thirty-eight-year-old Admiralty
clerk, was already serving an
eighteen-year sentence for
passing information to Russia
when he was driven on 28
January 1963 to attend the
Radcliffe tribunal which was
investigating security defects.

304
Christine Keeler,
twenty-four-year-old model,
was at the centre of the
Profumo affair in 1963, a
sensational scandal involving a
Cabinet Minister that rocked
the Macmillan government on
its heels.

305
The crush inside the
Government's Stationery
Office, Kingsway, London, as
people fought to buy first
copies of Lord Denning's
report on the security aspects
of the Profumo affair. The office
was specially opened
half-an-hour after midnight on
26 September 1963 for the sale
of the report.

306
The newspaper posters in
Petticoat Lane Market
proclaim the preoccupations of
a nation one Sunday morning in
1963: 'I knew Philby' by
Malcolm Muggeridge (The
Sunday Telegraph); 'The girls
of London's sweet life set – a
startling report names them all'
(*The People*); 'Christine talks'
(*News of the World*); while in
The *Sunday Times*, Angus
Maude writes, inevitably,
about 'The Middle-Class
Dilemma'.

307
On the night of 8 August 1963
the Great Train Robbery
resulted in the loss of £2,500,000
in used bank notes. Thirty
people took part in the raid and
the sheer audacity (together
with the subsequent escape
from prison of Ronald Biggs,
one of the robbers) won a
certain admiration for the
criminals. The injury to the train
driver and the fact that little of
the money was recovered did
not altogether kill this
admiration. Here, the guilty
men look out of the windows of
a Black Maria, 26 March 1964.

308
Sir Alec Douglas-Home was to
lead the Conservatives for a
short while in 1963–4. He seems
undaunted by the fact that
Labour has won the General
Election of October 1964.

309
Labour won the General
Election in 1964, surprisingly
by only five seats. Harold
Wilson was the youngest Prime
Minister of the century. With
his wife and son he drove in
triumph to Buckingham Palace
on 16 October 1964 for an
audience with the Queen.

310
The nation grieved at the death of Sir Winston Churchill who, as a commoner, was accorded the rare honour of a state funeral in January 1965.

311
Edward Heath took over the Conservative leadership in 1965, and joins Mr Reginald Maudling for a short walk towards St James's Park.

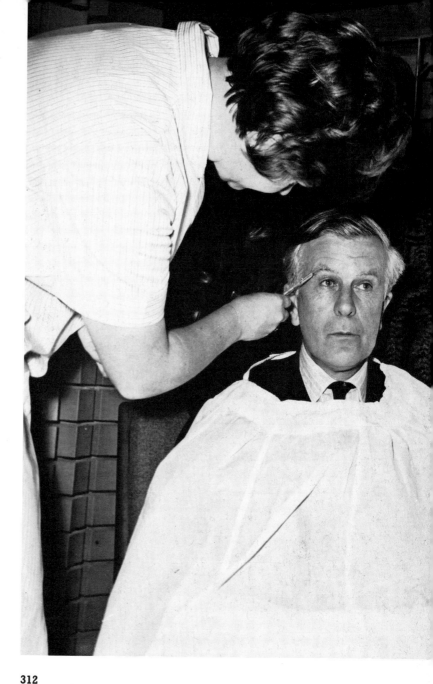

312
In the television age
appearance became
important. Jo Grimond, leader
of the Liberal Party, sits
patiently whilst a make-up girl
puts the final touches,
February 1966.

313
The terrible scene of death and
destruction as rescue workers
dig desperately into the vast
river of black, oozing
coal-slack that avalanched
down a Welsh mountainside on
22 October 1966, engulfing
houses and the village school of
the tiny mining village of
Aberfan, near Merthyr Tydfil,
South Wales.

314
English football's proudest
moment – Bobby Moore,
captain of England's successful
team in the 1966 World Cup,
holds aloft the Jules Rimet
trophy.

315
Sport was not only for the
young. At the age of 66, having
sailed around the world
singlehanded, Francis
Chichester was knighted on
7 July 1967.

316
Harold Wilson's longest-running crisis concerned Rhodesia. In December 1966 Wilson met Rhodesian Prime Minister, Ian Smith, aboard HMS *Tiger* in the Mediterranean to decide the independence issue. In his famous Gannex coat Harold Wilson stands by as Ian Smith leaves the *Tiger* after two days of talks which failed to resolve the crisis.

317
Another 'crisis' which went on and on was Britain's entry to the Common Market. De Gaulle still says 'Non' to Harold Wilson and Foreign Secretary George Brown on 25 January 1967.

318
Jo Grimond made way as leader of the Liberal Party for the informal, witty Jeremy Thorpe, 31 January 1967.

319
In Aden, the inhabitants ran
through the town on 3 April
1967 waving anti-British
banners and chanting
nationalist slogans. The Royal
Northumberland Fusiliers
retaliated in their own way.

320
Colonel Colin Campbell
Mitchell ('Mad Mitch'),
commanding officer of the
Argyll & Sutherland
Highlanders, takes his men
back into the Crater area of
Aden which had been sealed
off, July 1967.

321
A large crowd assembled at
Clydebank on 20 September
1967, and cheered loudly when
they heard the Queen say, 'I
name this ship the *Queen
Elizabeth 2*. May God bless her
and all who sail in her'.

322
Britain's defences crumble
sadly as the old London Bridge
is dismantled for its dispatch to
its new site – a tourist park in
Lake Havasu City, Arizona,
USA, 18 November 1968.

323
The *Torrey Canyon* aground off
Land's End in March 1967,
releasing a flood-tide of oil as
well as a massive public outcry
about environment.

324
The Ronan Point disaster in
1968 led people to question the
whole policy of high-rise
building. Where Britons had
lived so high how could the
quality of life be so low?

325
Concorde 001, a joint
Anglo-French venture, lifts off
the runway at Toulouse,
France, on her maiden flight, at
3.30 pm, 2 March 1969.

326
On 1 July 1969, Prince Charles
became Prince of Wales and
the links of the United Kingdom
were strengthened. Wearing a
gold coronet and ermine robe
and carrying a gold rod, the
Prince of Wales, the Queen
and the Duke of Edinburgh,
Princess Anne, the Queen
Mother and Princess Margaret
leave Caernarvon Castle by
the Water Gate after the
Investiture ceremonies.